MERCURY
The Smallest of All

by Chaya Glaser

Consultant: Karly M. Pitman, PhD
Planetary Science Institute
Tucson, Arizona

BEARPORT PUBLISHING

New York, New York

Credits

Cover, © NASA/APL; TOC, © NASA/APL; 4–5, © NASA/APL; 6–7, © Wikipedia & NASA; 8, © NASA/Johns Hopkins University; 9, © NASA; 10–11, © NASA/Johns Hopkins University; 12–13, © Jeffrey Beall/NASA; 14, © NASA/Johns Hopkins University; 15, © NASA/SDO (AIA); 16, © NASA/SDO (AIA); 17, © NASA/Johns Hopkins University; 18–19, © Carlos Clarivan/Science Photo Library; 20–21, © NASA/JHU/APL; 22TL, © NASA/Johns Hopkins University; 22TR, © NASA; 23TL, © NASA/JHUAPL/ Smithsonian Institution/Carnegie Institution of Washington; 23TM, © Wikipedia & NASA; 23TR, © Carlos Clarivan/Science Photo Library; 23BL, © NASA/JHU/APL; 23BR, © iStockphoto/Thinkstock; 24, © NASA/APL.

Publisher: Kenn Goin
Senior Editor: Joyce Tavolacci
Creative Director: Spencer Brinker
Design: Debrah Kaiser
Photo Researcher: Michael Win

Library of Congress Cataloging-in-Publication Data

Glaser, Chaya, author.
  Mercury : the smallest of all / by Chaya Glaser.
     pages cm. — (Out of this world)
  Includes bibliographical references and index.
  ISBN 978-1-62724-561-6 (library binding) — ISBN 1-62724-561-8 (library binding)
  1. Mercury (Planet)—Juvenile literature. I. Title.
  QB611.G53 2015
  523.41—dc23

                                    2014037333

For more information, write to Bearport Publishing Company, Inc., 45 West 21st Street, Suite 3B, New York, New York 10010. Printed in the United States of America.

10 9 8 7 6 5 4 3 2 1

CONTENTS

What's the smallest planet in our **Solar System?**

Mercury is the closest
planet to the Sun.

JUPiTER

MARS

VENUS

EARTH

MERCURY

SUN

6

SATURN

URANUS

NEPTUNE

The planet is much smaller than Earth.

MERCURY

Seventeen Mercurys could fit inside Earth.

EARTH

Mercury is covered with rocky craters.

They look like giant round bowls.

Craters

Sometimes, people can see Mercury from Earth.

It looks like a dot in the night sky.

Mercury

During the day, Mercury is very hot.

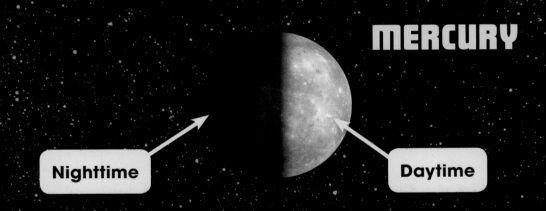

MERCURY

Nighttime

Daytime

Its temperature can reach 800°F (427°C)!

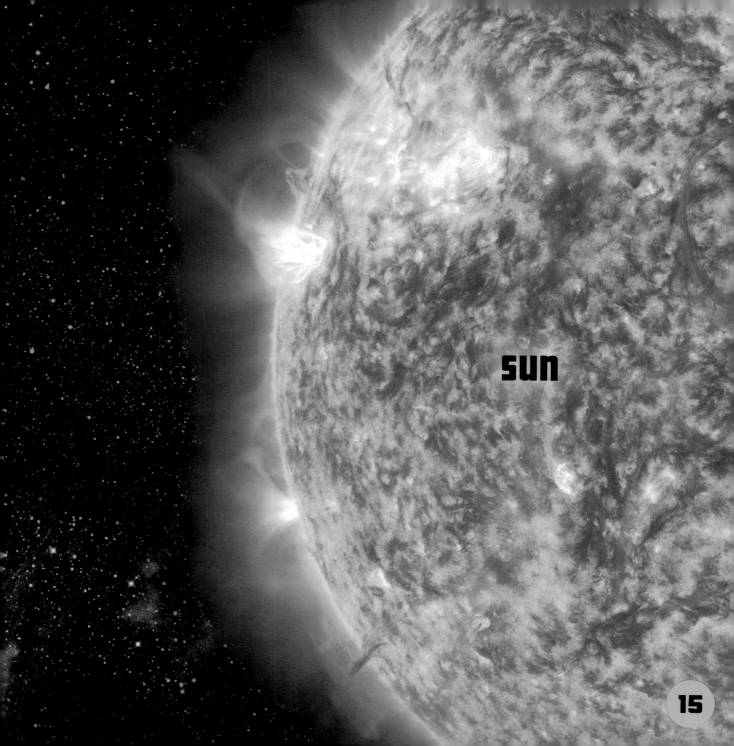

sun

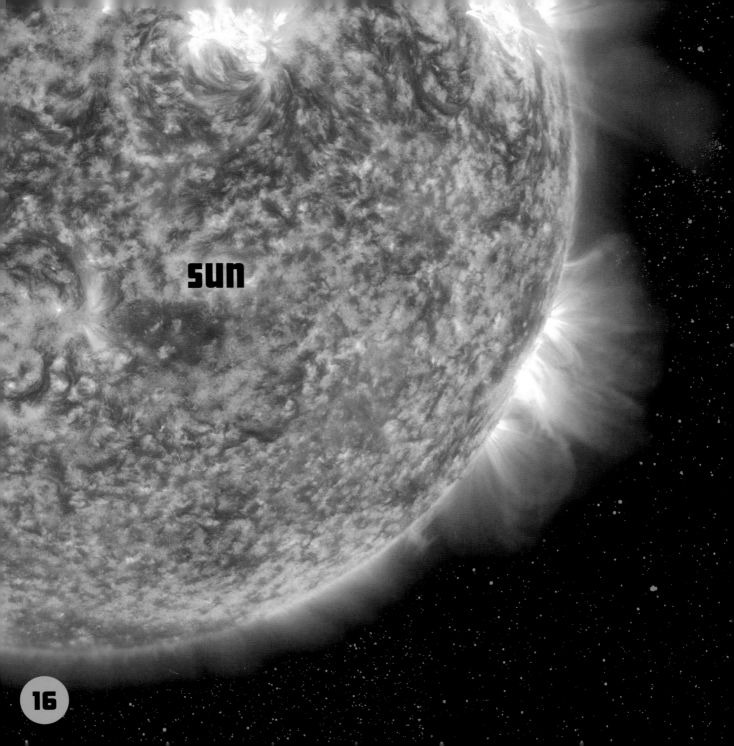

sun

At night, the temperature drops.

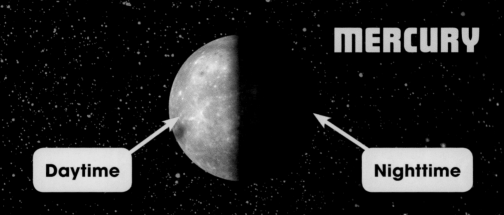

MERCURY

Daytime

Nighttime

It falls to a freezing –290°F (–179°C).

sun

Two **spacecraft** have visited Mercury.

They took photos of the planet.

To get to Mercury, they flew close to the Sun.

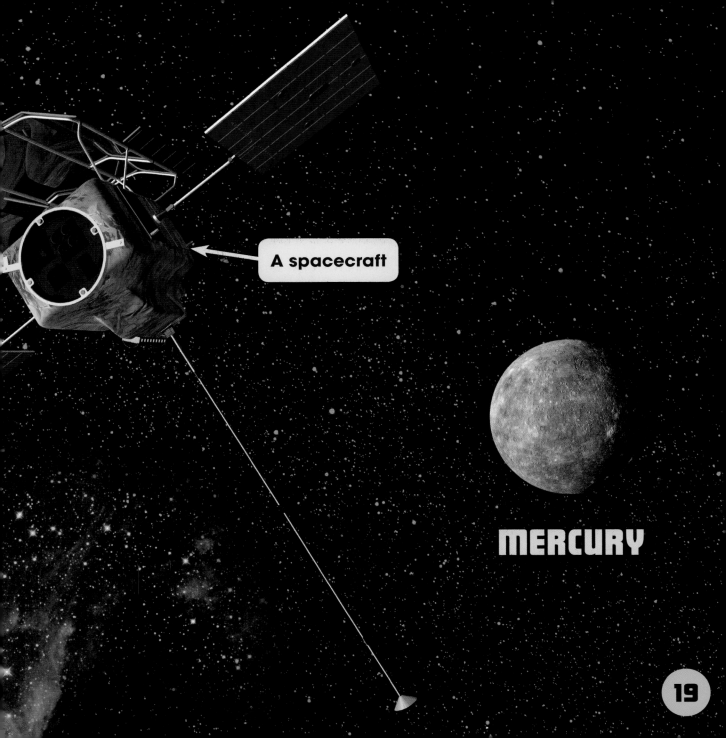

A spacecraft

MERCURY

sun

The spacecraft had special sunshades.

The shades protected the spacecraft from the Sun's heat.

They made sure the spacecraft didn't burn up!

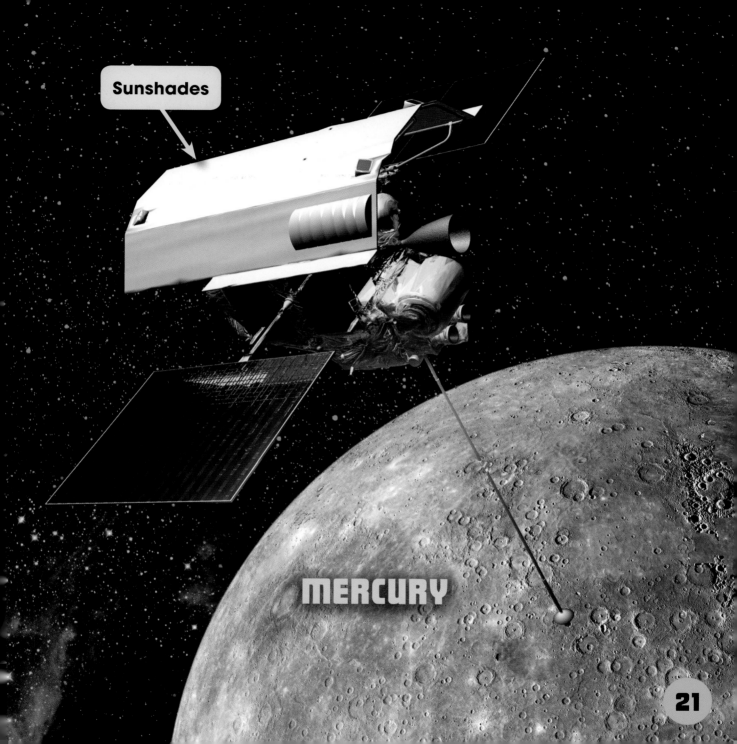

MERCURY VERSUS EARTH

MERCURY	POSITION	EARTH
First planet from the Sun	**POSITION**	Third planet from the Sun
3,032 miles (4,879 km) across	**SIZE**	7,918 miles (12,743 km) across
About 354°F (179°C)	**AVERAGE TEMPERATURE**	59°F (15°C)
Zero	**NUMBER OF MOONS**	One
Mostly rock with craters	**SURFACE**	Mostly ocean with some land

GLOSSARY

craters (KRAY-turs) large holes in the ground

Solar System (SOH-lur SISS-tuhm) the Sun and everything that circles around it, including the eight planets

spacecraft (SPAYSS-kraft) vehicles that can travel in space

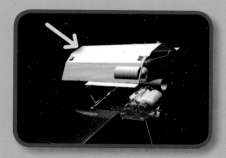

sunshades (SUN-shayds) something used as protection from the Sun's heat

temperature (TEM-pur-uh-chur) how hot or cold something is

INDEX

READ MORE

Lawrence, Ellen. *Mercury: The High-Speed Planet (Zoom Into Space).* New York: Ruby Tuesday Books (2014).

Taylor-Butler, Christine. *Mercury (Scholastic News Nonfiction Readers).* New York: Children's Press (2008).

LEARN MORE ONLINE

To learn more about Mercury, visit
www.bearportpublishing.com/OutOfThisWorld

ABOUT THE AUTHOR

Chaya Glaser enjoys looking up at the stars and reading stories about the constellations. When she's not admiring the night sky, she can be found playing musical instruments.